MASTERING
WEALTH AND HAPPINESS
12 ESSENTIALS RULES FOR SUCCESS

STRATEGIES FOR SUCCESS
AND FULFILLMENT

YOUR GUIDE
TO WEALTH AND
HAPPINESS

J. F. GUCO

ISBN: 9798873568390

TABLE OF CONTENTS

DEDICATION

To my beloved family, an unwavering foundation in my journey towards understanding and the tireless search for true wealth and happiness. Throughout the years, they have been more than my loved ones; they have been my invaluable companions, generously sharing their wisdom and joys, and walking beside me at every crossroads and challenge of life.

This book, my humble contribution to knowledge and reflection, is dedicated in a special way to each of you. The dedication goes beyond words, it is a sincere recognition for your unconditional support, your constant love and the strength you bring to my daily existence.

May these pages, born of heart and shared experience, serve as a lasting reminder that success and joy are achievements we celebrate together as a family. May this book be an additional bond that strengthens our family bond, reminding us of the importance of supporting each other on our journey toward personal fulfillment.

With deep appreciation and eternal affection,

J.F. GUCO."

ACKNOWLEDGMENTS

At the culmination of this project, I wish to express my deep gratitude to those who have contributed invaluably to the creation of this book.

To my family, for your constant support and unconditional love. Each one of you has been my rock, my motivation and my reason to aspire for more.

To my friends, whose friendship has been a treasure over the years. Thank you for being a source of inspiration, for the conversations that challenged my thoughts and for sharing laughs that lightened the path.

To the readers who entrust their time and attention to these pages, I sincerely hope you find inspiration and valuable lessons that will enrich your lives.

Finally, I thank life itself for giving me the experiences that have shaped this journey of learning and growth.

With gratitude, J. F. GUCO

INTRODUCTION

M uch has been written and in different ways, to improve our life, to have money, to be rich. But very few have followed the advice, why, I don't know.

Perhaps many of you are apathetic, afraid to face another reality, or in fact, you are conformists.

This is for you, who have the desire to excel, and I say it is for you, because from the moment you have these rules in your hands, it is because you have the desire to be rich.

But don't think it is easy, it is necessary to have a lot of desire and faith, and dedicate a little of your time to the simple rules, because to receive you must first give something in return, do not think that things will fall from the sky.

Are you ready to move forward or not yet?

Are you fearful, cowardly, pusillanimous or conformist, I don't think so.

But if you are, I give you a piece of advice, don't read on, find a trash can and throw these rules away, because you will never understand them and you will not carry them out as they should be.

I challenge you to carry out the following rules, in this way, engrave in your mind, that like eating, you breathe the rules daily, at least for thirty days each one of them, likewise, you will read them three times in the same day, if you do not believe you are capable of doing it, do not do it, forget it, continue your life as you have been living it until now, you do not deserve anything else.

But if you have the desire to improve yourself, follow them, and you will see that little by little life offers a number of nuances and opportunities that you do not know, for the simple reason that you want to and not because you have been forbidden; because through time life has taught us that there are winners and losers.

Which group of people do you belong to?

Think a little and you will find the solution.

Now, think about which group of people you want to belong to, the victors or simply the defeated.

Perfect! To the victors. So let's move on.

You may ask yourself: What should I do or perform. The answer is very simple.

The answer lies in your mind and in your person, and you are the possessor of the answer. It is in you, but it is you need to discover it, to find the real and true meaning of the answer.

I will only try to guide you to find it.

You have in your hands, my rules, easy and simple for be rich and happy.

Please reason them, understand them and you will be rich and happy.

It is essential that you stop your regrets, because they do not lead you to positive paths and only create obstacles.

By lamenting, you do not solve anything, on the contrary, you only torment yourself and your thoughts are fixed on it.

Free yourself from this torment, start now to change, start thinking positively.

Set a goal to reach, or several goals, set them higher and higher than normal and try to reach them, because if you choose the right path, with your decision and faith in yourself, it will be very easy to reach them, and you will say later, how easy this is and how difficult it was for me before.

Remember your past, try to erase from your mind the bad things that have happened to you, keep for yourself only the beautiful things you have enjoyed, the achievements you have reached, because only these will help you to reach better achievements.

The failures you have had, forget them, but always keep in mind that you must not repeat them, for you would be foolish to do so.

Do not be afraid of life, it is very beautiful, enjoy it in all its splendor because in it, you will also find the answer to wealth and happiness.

Love your fellow men as you love yourself, do not despise the humble, the rich, the beautiful, the ugly, the strong or the weak, because in them you will find qualities that you may not possess, observe them, study them, listen to them and take advantage of them, of the virtues they possess and of their assimilated failures, so that you do not incur in the same.

So, let's go for it!

"Before I continue, I want to share with you these rules for wealth and happiness. They were taught to me with love and respect, passed down from generation to generation. Personally, I have found success and satisfaction in applying them, and have passed them on to my children. Now, with affection, I share them with you. If you find value in them, I encourage you to share them with friends".

So, I tell you again: GO FORWARD!

FIRST RULE

WHO ARE YOU?

Have I ever wondered who I am?

Yes or no, what conclusion did I reach? Do I really know myself?

It is necessary for me to know myself, to observe my virtues but also my defects.

How will I do this? It is very simple.

I must first get to know my body to know who I am. And how will I do that?

It's easy.

Every morning when I get up and before I take a bath, I will look at myself in the mirror for at least five minutes, I will observe my hair, my eyes, my lips, my hands, my feet, my calluses, my moles, in short, everything that my body has, and after a week of observing myself, I will begin to write down the things that I like most about my body, and in the same way, I will write down the things that I don't like about my body. At least ten of each of these observations.

And what does this lead me to? It's easy to guess.

(I have not realized) that when I find the things that I like and dislike about my body, is when I will really learn to know myself physically, and I will begin to take care of the details of my body, and by taking care of the details I will begin to love myself more, since I will examine and take care of everything I use to apply to my body, because I must take care of it, because it is beautiful, beautiful, and if I do not take care of it, who will? No one, I must learn to love it, I must not hurt it but on the contrary, love it, I will not hurt it because if I hurt myself, I do not love myself, and if I do not love myself I do not love anyone, I must learn to love myself and a lot to love all those who love me around me, and even those I do not know, for someday I will know them.

Why I will do all this, it is very simple, because I still do not know who I am, everything I do is routine, it is washing, drying, dressing, grooming, and so on, but I have lost the grace of knowing who I am, because I do not observe myself, indeed, I think, I no longer have time. I must steal five minutes of my time and use them to observe myself to know who I am, in this way I will learn to love myself a lot and when I achieve it, I will finally know what I can expect from life, because I will finally love myself and I will know who I am.

Because, in reality, I am a great being, who has in this life a task to fulfill, for which I will strive day by day, minute by minute, second by second, until I accomplish it, until I fulfill it.

Because knowing myself, I will know who I am, where I am going and what I want in this life, or maybe I do not want anything, if it is this, then I will do nothing, I will not know myself, I will not sculpt my body and I will simply be another parasite on this earth, where I will only cause disgust, revulsion, fear, by the other people who see me and surround me. If I do not know how to love myself, I will not know how to love anyone and I should never expect to be loved, without being surprised if I am also hurt.

Once I know the things that I like and dislike about myself, I will start to think carefully, why I like certain parts of my body? in the same way, I will think a little more, why there are things that I dislike about my body? and I will put all my attention on them, because these things I must improve them, I must compose them, I must polish them, since, to everything I possess I must give good use, and I will put all my attention on them, because I must improve these things, I must improve them, I must polish them, because I must give good use to everything I possess, and with this, I will also come to love them until finally, everything I possess in my body I will learn to love it and to give it good use, and when I give it the proper use, I will know myself, I will know who I am, and I will know what I want from this life.

I must remember at every moment that those who despise themselves are despised by others, and those who love themselves are loved by others.

SECOND RULE.

WHERE ARE YOU GOING?

Have I ever thought about where I come from, where I am going, what I really want from this life or what really belongs to me and how I should get it?

This is the easiest thing to do.

I am a product of love, of the union of two beings who in a divine moment conceived me, and who from before I was born, already loved me, and I, still unconscious, already loved them.

From that moment on, I learned to love myself, since I unconsciously tried by all means within my reach to survive, to respond to his caresses, his pampering and his sadness for me.

And today, that I am grown up, I have forgotten the most important thing in my life, which is, to know where I am going.

Isn't it true that when I was not yet born, the most important thing in my existence was to be born, isn't it true that at that moment, I already knew where I was going?

And today; with the passage of time, I have lost the compass to find my way.

I must think and think a lot about where I am going, what I want, where I will guide my steps and not where my steps will guide me, and this is the most important thing in my life, because if my mind does not dominate my steps, I will surely stumble and fall into the abyss and if I have already fallen into it, I must think about how to get out of it, I remember when I was not yet born, that what I most wanted in the world was to be born and to live.

Today, I am alive, and I must remain so, and I must learn to know and know where I am going, what I want.

Then, I am alive.

I must learn to live. I want to be rich.

But, this is only words, I really want and wish to be alive, and what should I do, first, I will take care of myself, I will try by all means to avoid being hurt.

I must also learn to live, and this is easy, life gives me satisfactions that I take from it, and each one of them I must enjoy to the maximum, because a being, supreme creator, has given it to me and I must not waste it, on the contrary, I must make the most of it in my favor.

I want to be rich.

I think where I am going, what I want; but I must think with great force having a great desire to be rich and I will be rich, that at this moment I possess the wealth of being alive, while others are dead, that

I do not have the joy of being breathing when others are no longer breathing?

I must learn to know where I am going and what I want, and I am going to wealth and I want to be immensely rich, and I will be, because by thinking, by means of the mind this stream of ideas that flow endlessly, will make me immensely rich and I will be.

But I must not fail, I do not want to be a failure in this life, on the contrary, I want to be a winner, and I will be if I know how to guide my steps along the right paths of life.

If in the past I misguided my steps and they led me to failure, today I commit myself to redirect my path along the enlightened path of bliss, happiness and victory.

With the lessons learned from my mistakes, I understand that every setback is an opportunity to grow and improve.

From now on, regardless of my role in life, I will always adopt a positive approach.

My thoughts will be steeped in optimism, rejecting any hint of negativity that might stand in my way. I am determined to build a future where success will crown my persistent efforts.

Every day will be a new opportunity to learn, evolve and move towards my goals with determination. I believe in the ability to transform challenges into opportunities, and I am ready to embrace the success that will result from my commitment to positive thinking and diligent action.

THIRD RULE

WATCH

D o I observe?

I have lost the grace of observing worldly life, it has taken away the grace of observing above my head, and I only see where my feet tread.

I must stop to observe. The houses, the streets, the trees, the sky and everything, but I must not only look but observe, I must learn to observe, learn, because the things I observe have life even if I don't believe it, everything has life and is there for a reason and with observation I will learn why it is there.

I have to think about why certain things were put in that place.

I have to think about who made it possible for that thing to be there.

I must think how much work and sacrifice the things that surround us have, because each thing that surrounds us has a history, and that history, I will try to imagine how it is, I will only decipher it by observing.

I must observe the men and women who pass around me, and observe them well, to try to know what they think, what they want, what can be useful to them, what they need, in short, many things that only by observing I will discover.

And if I find out what they need, I will give them what they ask for, but in return I will charge, here is a rule to start my career, to be rich, because I will be, but the money will not come to my hands fallen from the sky, on the contrary, I must know who I am, where I am going, and I must observe, to be able to translate my most fervent desire into money and be able to be rich and happy.

By observing, I will learn to love nature, what surrounds me, and those around me, because all the things that surround me are beautiful, and to find the beauty that they hide I will only achieve it by observing, and I will finally know the practical utility that I can give them, for the benefit of others, and mainly, for my own benefit.

Since, by giving satisfactions to others, I will give myself satisfactions mainly, which I will translate into money and which, in a very short time, will give me more money; for this reason, I must learn to observe, this is a skill that I have lost, but I have lost it because I wanted to, by leaving aside, forgotten, the grace of observation.

From now on I make a firm resolution to go back to carefully observing everything around me, what is above my head, to observe nature which is so beautiful, and to find my own benefit from everything I observe for myself.

I must imitate those who have succeeded, with the grace of observation, for this grace is not only reserved to them, I also have the right and the faculty to observe, and this I will do from now on.

By observing, I will discover the beautiful things in life, I will discover what people need, their tastes and their desires, in short! What they want, and that is where I will try to give them a service.

By observing, I will also perfect and improve the work I do and develop it with more love, as if this were a vice to which I am accustomed.

Because work does not debase, on the contrary, it perfects man and makes him great.

That is how I want to be, great, successful, and I will be because it is my strongest desire and I must achieve it, I will not stay half way, I will achieve everything and only then will I be rich and happy.

I must always keep in mind that I must learn to observe everything around me, and observe it well, not half-heartedly.

FOURTH RULE

LEARN

From my failures and defeats, what have I learned, nothing, I am wrong. I have learned not to make the same mistakes so as not to fail and be defeated.

There is an animal, the donkey, that when you pass it on a path and it does not trip over a stone, you can pass it again on that same path, in front of that same stone hundreds of times and it will not trip over it, just imagine, it is a donkey and it knows that. What do I know?

I know who I am. Where am I going?

I have already learned to observe?

And from observation I must learn what those around me need, and I must learn to do it well, for what I offer them must please them, be useful to them, and in that way I will acquire more money than I ever dreamed of.

It is not necessary to have an extraordinary culture to learn to be intelligent, too intelligent, to have a university degree, nonsense, these are the ones who have less money compared to those who learn by observing, have I not noticed that the great majority of university students work for others, that they become bureaucrats in public and private offices, have they become fearful, apathetic and conformist? They have become fearful, apathetic and conformist, many employees and workers are also fearful, apathetic and conformist.

Me, I don't want to be like them, no.

Therefore, I must learn from observation to free my mind, so that it starts to develop and think a little bit more than usual, I must improve everything I do, improve what I already do, give it a better finish, I must improve myself and this, I know how, I can't with material things, of course I can!

Observing, I will find fault with everything and I will try to improve it, and by doing it better everything will be easier, I must learn to use my mind more than my physical strength.

Because I don't want to be a loader all my life or drag a yoke of oxen. No.

I must think, how to learn by observing and improving the things around me, with less physical efforts than others do, here is another rule of my life, by observing I will learn, since I know who I am and where I am going.

I must not be lazy to think, on the contrary, I must learn to think, I must exercise my mind all the time, every day, and this is not tiring, it is simple.

Do I get tired from breathing, from eating, do I not? Then I must learn and observe, in short, I must perfect the little I know, learning, always learning to think and perfect the little or much I know.

I will learn from the mistakes I have made and the mistakes my peers have made, over time.

The whole of humanity has made mistakes, but I must not carry them with me; on the contrary, I must assimilate them, so as not to make them again.

If it is necessary to acquire and learn specialized knowledge, I will train in them; in our country, there are a variety of public and private schools that provide specialized training, and there are online schools, I can resort to them and if I have the desire to improve myself day by day, I will go to them.

"I will orient my learning towards the practical realm of life, recognizing the importance of applying the knowledge acquired. What would be the use of accumulating wisdom if I do not put it into practice?

I will dedicate my daily efforts to continually learn and improve myself, with the objective of obtaining benefits for both myself and my family. I understand that personal growth not only impacts my own life, but also the lives of others. It is through this constant commitment that I aspire to achieve my goals: to be a prosperous and happy person. And I am convinced that, with effort and dedication, I will achieve it."

FIFTH RULE

SAVE

Have I ever really saved in my life?

Nothing of the sort, everything I have earned, the little I have thought I have saved, I have spent. I have forgotten a simple rule, that saving is the basis of capital.

This, I mean:

That from now on, from what I earn, I intend to save as much as I can, in a day, in a week, in a month. And I must forget about the money I save. And I must put the money I save to work so that it will produce profits for me, and the profits, I must also save them and not touch them for some time.

I take a solemn oath to save and invest what I manage to save for a period of five years, and at the end of that time I will see the results.

It is not difficult to save; the simplest rule is just to set your mind to it.

And this, I propose myself from this moment, everything I can save from what I earn, I will save it; I will not throw my money in buying things that do not serve for nothing, since this is garbage, things that at the moment have caught my attention, but that really do not serve for nothing.

Why should I throw my money away on things that are useless, why should I let myself be persuaded to buy things I don't need, why should I let myself be persuaded to buy things I don't need?

Only because they are proposed to me, because they invite me to do so!

From now on, I will not listen to the special offers that are offered to me, because these offers and those who offer them to me, want to take my money, and I will not let them, since they are the ones who do not want me to be rich and prosperous.

I must instill in myself daily the habit of saving, from this moment on I will only buy what is indispensable and necessary for me and my family, I must not buy junk, since it is just that, junk.

And when I learn this simple rule, I will begin to see the results and fruits of my efforts.

Since it is an effort, since all those around me have accustomed me not to save, to spend the money I earn and even more, to spend more than I earn, going into debt for months, for years paying high interest and this is a step that has no end and if I must, I will try to save some of what I have left over, as much as I can, since only in this way, I will reach wealth.

I must never forget that saving is the basis of capital.

I must remember that people who today have wealth is because they know the simple rule of saving, and for that reason, now they have money, but I must also remember that in the beginning they did not have a single penny, they only had a firm determination, which was to save and that became a habit, and today they have a lot of money, money that today gives them many satisfactions and that tomorrow I will also have, because from today on I will have only one purpose in my life, which will be the habit of saving and together with my other determinations when I finally learn to save, I will no longer worry about tomorrow because, with the saved product I will have secured peace of mind, food and other things for the family and for me.

The task of saving is greatly simplified when we set out to discipline ourselves. It is a matter of reminding myself, over and over again, that the act of saving is not a difficult task, but rather a habit that grows stronger with practice and repetition.

Whenever I feel the urge to buy something that has only momentarily captured my attention, I must remember that it is important to resist temptation and avoid spending my money on superfluous things that will ultimately bring no real benefit.

Keeping in my mind the idea that saving is an essential part of my financial routine will help me make more conscious decisions and recognize the value of every penny earned.

Each saving represents a personal achievement, the result of my hard work and dedication, so I must never forget the importance of allocating a portion of my earnings to savings.

This practice not only contributes to my personal financial well-being, but also reflects the fruit of my individual effort and my commitment to a stronger and more stable future.

SIXTH RULE

LOVE

"If you want to be loved, you must first learn to love yourself, so that with cleanness of heart you may love your fellow men.

I must forget the rancor and hatred that I once professed for any of my fellow men, and in my inner fire, I must learn to love all my fellow men.

But this is not simple, because for me to have the gift of love I must first learn to love myself, and this I will do in a simple way.

I know myself, I know who I am, I don't like to hurt myself, in times past I have caused myself harm and allowed others to harm me, but now I am no longer willing or accepting to harm myself, neither for myself nor for others.

On the contrary, today more than ever I must take care of myself because I love myself, I am a being created by love, and I am in this world to love myself and to love others.

I must remember that love is the main basis of this life, since it would be impossible to live with hatred and resentment, because my heart would wither and die.

Therefore, if I want to live, I must do so with love and joy, that my heart be free of grudges and hatred.

I must love myself, take care of myself as the greatest and most sublime treasure that God has given me.

I must scrupulously watch over the care of my person, the clothes I wear, because this will be the reflection of my heart and the confidence I give to others.

I must not cause harm to anyone and much less to my family, I must love them much more, since I spend a great part of my time with them, we share food and a roof, therefore the moments when we are together must be the most beautiful in life.

I must listen to their problems, their laments, their joys, to be able to live day by day with greater love and happiness, because as long as I have tranquility and peace in my home, I will do my work without pressure of any nature, and I will do it in the best possible way, and this will give me an economic result of greater benefit to me and my family, and eventually I will be rich and happy, which is the goal I have set for myself in life.

The rule for success is work, which must be done with love, abnegation, passion and joy.

SEVENTH RULE.

DEFINE

Rectify your path, define the steps to follow.

The steps I have taken so far have not led me to wealth.

Why?

Perhaps, because they were poorly managed.

It is necessary, from now on, to define the objective that I have set for myself in this life, and it is necessary to define my objective.

What do I want?

I want to be rich, to have a lot of money, I must think about that and have faith.

Above all, I must have faith in myself and this can only be achieved by knowing myself, by loving myself, because by loving myself I will learn to love all mankind.

Every morning, when I get up, I will channel my steps to success, to improve my personal relationships with all the people I deal with, for therein lies another primordial rule to become rich.

I must determine that what I want is to earn money, having faith, mainly, in myself.

Determining my absolute desire to be rich.

I must conclude my fervent desire to be rich, and I will be.

Why have others been able to be and not me? Because they have determined their steps to wealth and have concluded them.

When I start my workday, I must finish what I have set out to do, if I do not, I will be a failure, and I do not want to belong to the group of failures.

I must be among the winners, and I will be a winner, I will be rich.

I should not waste time in things that do not produce me, on the contrary, I will occupy my time and if necessary a little more of it, in producing, working, since work does not debase, but on the contrary, it ennobles, ennobles, strengthens, dignifies and gives us the recognition of all those around us.

I must use action in everything I undertake, conclude my steps even if I believe that it will be very difficult to achieve it, because this is a lie, since with action and determination in concluding what I start, nothing is difficult and everything is easy for me.

Define your actions, your work plan, what you plan to do, analyze it and try to carry it out.

But first, set a well-defined goal to know what you want and where you are going.

Do not start anything if you do not know where you are going, because this would be like walking aimlessly through the streets, through the countryside, anywhere, without knowing where you are going.

In such a way, you must always know what you want and where you are going, for only in this way will you obtain the wealth and happiness that are yours in your own right.

Don't drift through the world like a rudderless ship.

Define your path. What you want, where you are going, where you will get to, what you will do.

What do you want? To succeed, to be rich and happy.

Where are you going? Towards success, wealth and happiness.

Where will you go? Wherever you propose if you are physically and mentally prepared for it, and you will reach the peak of triumph, wealth and happiness.

What I will do, I will do my best, I will put all my heart and enthusiasm to do my job, I will always keep in mind that I will bear the effort of the job as if it were a game, besides, I will work, thinking that my job is a vice for me.

For by doing my work to the best of my ability, I will succeed, I will achieve the wealth and happiness that is mine.

Therefore, I will always define my path and work before I start, so as not to stumble upon failure, since I am not willing to fail again.

RULE EIGHT

FE

Have faith in everything you do, especially have faith in yourself.

Have you forgotten that faith can move mountains?

I must learn to have faith in myself, to have faith in everything I do.

I will teach my mind that the faith I profess to myself is the greatest and most sublime thing in life.

With faith in myself, I will be able to carry out any kind of work that I develop, because, having faith in myself, I will stop being afraid.

Because if I am afraid, it is because I have no faith in myself, and I believe I am incapable of doing any job, no matter how simple it may be.

But I, I have faith in myself, in my person and in what I possess, and with faith I will triumph and overcome all the obstacles that are put in my way, to prevent me from triumphing. But that will be impossible, because I have faith in myself and therefore, I will triumph.

With faith, I will reach the highest rungs of life and attain unsuspected riches.

Faith will give me determination to carry out any work I develop.

I must have faith that I will soon be rich and happy, engrave it in my mind, so that it will be so.

And what is faith? It is the power of thought. This means that I must channel my thinking to positive things, so that my actions are positive, everything bad must be evicted by my thinking because it will not lead me to anything good, and in the long run, it will only cause me problems and I will suffer.

Therefore, by means of my mind and thought, I can channel my steps to wealth and happiness, for this, with the power of my mind and thought, I must command myself, and I will auto-suggest that I will be rich and happy. And I will be.

But not only is autosuggestion necessary, discipline is also necessary, this means that when we are with sufficiently strong faith, towards the path to wealth and happiness, we must also set ourselves, mentally, a discipline to follow in order to chain our steps and not lose the path to wealth and happiness.

You must engrave in your mind that to obtain wealth and happiness, FAITH is your starting point.

Learn that the constant repetition of positive thinking, will make you act positively, that is, you must learn to order yourself through the mind, what do you want from this life, what is the goal you have set, what do you want to have, record all this in your mind and to help it, make a list of what you want, however unlikely it may seem, and every morning and evening, daily, you must learn to read it and think about it, and you will notice how easy and simple the things you have written on the list will be accomplished.

Therefore, you must not forget that faith moves mountains, and that faith is the force of thought and action.

In such a way, combine your thought with action, so that you will have enough faith that you will succeed in what you have proposed, and in your goals, drawn on your paper and in your mind, the faith that you will reach the goal that will lead you to wealth and happiness.

RULE NINE

BE PRACTICAL

I should not complicate my life.

I must be practical.

Whatever work I do, I must be practical, I must not complicate the realization of my work, because this will take me time to do it, and what I need is time.

Time to develop more work, produce more, earn more, because I want to be rich; if I don't do this, I will never have enough money to be rich and I will be mediocre, I will be someone else who doesn't count among the people. I will be a nobody.

And I am tired of being a nobody, I want to be among the best, and for that, I must be practical, I must not compromise things no matter how difficult they may seem, because, certainly, there is nothing difficult in this life, even if I believe there is.

I must make a resolution to work harder every day and stop complicating the work I do.

This is a very simple rule that I must never forget, on the contrary, I must always keep it present in my mind and in my heart, I must be practical, only in this way I will succeed and be great with all my friends, and in this way, I will become rich, which is the path I am pursuing.

I must learn to be practical in everything I do, nothing is difficult, everything is easy if we have the faith and the desire for it to be so, and it will be so.

For no reason will I listen to those who advise me otherwise, because those people instead of being my friends, are my enemies, their desire is that I fail in the attempt I am making to be rich, what they want me not to be, they want me to remain a mediocre, a nobody, but that no longer enters into the plans of my life. I will succeed in life with another simple rule. That of being practical.

I will no longer complicate the things I do or my work, on the contrary, I must see them in the simplest possible way, and that is how it will be from now on.

Since the complications that I found to things in the past, have only been a product of my mind, and since this has been, from now on, my mind will make me see all things in the simplest possible way, I will achieve the triumph that I have proposed to myself, which is to be rich and happy.

From now on, I will begin to be practical, and everything I do will be easier and I will do it with the greatest joy that is in my heart, and in this way, I will achieve the goal that I have set for myself.

Practice makes perfect, therefore, remember your past, your achievements and successes, perfect them, and make them again with the practice and experience you have.

The practical, is what has greater acceptance among people, because they will never buy or accept complicated things, since they do not want to complicate their existence.

In such a way that the practical, is what has greater acceptance among the people, since it is easy, and if what I do, I complicate it, I will fail. But I must not accept failure, therefore, in everything I do I must be practical, to be a winner and achieve wealth and happiness, which are mine and belong to me.

I must never forget that being practical is the best thing I must have to succeed, and from now on, I will be practical and not complicated with the things I do or perform.

RULE TEN

ATACA

I must never accept defeat, on the contrary, I will always attack first to be victorious.

I am tired of being defeated, life has given me the instincts and strength to win, but I will only win if I attack before the others.

I must not forget: "He who strikes first strikes twice, or is this not true? Why should I wait to be struck first?

I must attack, and for this, I must think carefully my steps, in all cases, in every business that I undertake or to develop the work that I do. Always better than my other companions, because although when they tell me, do not make an effort, they do the opposite and only try to harm me, I must not listen to them, because they are not my friends, on the contrary, he who tries to harm me, is my enemy.

Every day when I get up, the first thing my mind will order is to attack, attack in my work, in what I do, in what I do, I will leave the place where I live with my mind well disposed to attack and not to let myself be attacked, so as not to be defeated by others, on the contrary, I will attack and dominate them with my perseverance, with my faith, with my love and thus, I will defeat them.

I will never again be defeated by others; on the contrary, I will defeat them and they will be the defeated.

From now on, I will always attack and win, and every time I win, it will be one more step towards the goal of wealth and happiness that I have set for myself in my life.

I will work harder, with more love, with more passion, which is the only way I know how to attack, and in this way, I will win. Yes, I will overcome the adversity that many times has pursued me and that I have not known how to attack it and overcome it, I will attack and overcome. This will be the idea that I will always have in my mind every day when I start working, in this way, I will win and I will never be defeated again.

I will stop being afraid of others, since in the past I was humiliated, despised and even made fun of me, this was because I was afraid of them, fear. Shame or respect, but from now on, I must learn that we are all equal so I am not afraid of anyone and what's more, all those I was afraid of I will defeat them and they will have to respect me, and so they will have to respect me.

Attack, remember how animals attack when they are hungry or when they are defending themselves.

You, you are hungry for wealth and happiness, therefore, you must attack, always reflect on your attitude before attacking your prey, the possible consequences of your gain, but attack, do not stay still, you should not be faint-hearted, fearful, on the contrary, you are strong of heart, of faith, of action and it is necessary that you attack, so you can succeed and achieve the wealth and happiness that are yours.

Defend yourself from the attacks of others, since they are also hungry for triumph, wealth and happiness, and if you let them defeat you, you will be defeated and they will be the victors, but you should not allow that; for that reason, defend yourself from aggression and attack to win and not be defeated, achieve wealth and happiness, which are yours and no one else's.

For this reason, you must always attack to achieve your objectives and the goals you have set, and reach them to their final consequence, do not leave them halfway because this will make you a failure and not a winner.

RULE ELEVEN

INVEST

From the proceeds of my savings, what should I do? Invest!

Oh, I don't know? Well, I must think, I must imagine things in which I can develop work on my own, increase money or capital, however small it may be, in order to increase it and own more, it is necessary that I have imagination, that I think, so that my brain works and orders me what I must do and thus, the intangible becomes a reality.

There are so many things that mankind needs as services, satisfiers and other products to satisfy their needs, that it is necessary and I intend to find out what they are, or what it is, so that I can start working on it.

I am not going to discover anything, maybe not, but what already exists, I am going to improve it, to perfect it with great care and affection, I will put all my effort into it, all my love, all my faith so that everything I do turns out well.

I must invest not only money, but also effort, capacity, time, desire, faith, love and decision to be able to realize what I desire, what I long for, and this becomes money and happiness, more money and more happiness day by day.

And from the profits I get, I will save and invest, since I should not spend my money on things that are not worthwhile, I will invest it, so that it will produce more and more for me.

I must be cautious in my investments, the great offers or stimuli of great businesses must be studied correctly, giving me enough time to think about them, since they can be a siren's song.

If I do not act correctly, all that I have gained I will lose and if this happens, I should not imagine that my life ends there, on the contrary, it begins again with a lesson and a great experience that I was cheated, and it will serve me to be better prepared, to start the road again, being more cautious and astute than the others.

I must not forget that the people who approach me to offer me to earn fabulous amounts, want to cheat me, because nobody is willing to share his earnings if he knows that they are safe, because if they are safe, he would not offer it to me, he would do the business alone and he would not share his earnings, otherwise, if he is not sure of his success, he would offer it to me so that I could go on an adventure with him, maybe the one who offers it to me is not interested but I am, I am not willing to lose a single cent of my property, because nobody gives money away and it is difficult and it takes a lot of work to earn it.

I must take care of my money, just as I take care of my life, my children, my wife, because only in this way will I understand that money is a satisfier that has the power to provide me with other satisfactions.

And if I want more comfort than I enjoy, I must make sure that what I invest, however little, is a safe investment, so as not to go on an adventure that will only leave me with sadness, bitterness and reproach.

There is currently no better way than to invest wisely what we have earned with so much sacrifice.

It is not fair that the effort we have made to achieve wealth and happiness should vanish from our hands.

Therefore, I must invest the proceeds of my earnings, in order to earn higher profits again.

I must think that there are currently a variety of good investments, such as: land, houses, bank deposits, businesses, investments, stock market and others, and I must think long and hard about what to invest in.

I should not allow advertising to influence my financial decisions; rather, I should critically analyze the available options. The key is to identify those investments that generate the highest returns with the lowest possible risk. Understanding that a bad investment can mean the loss of invested resources and, therefore, the restart of the process of accumulating wealth and happiness, underscores the importance of being meticulous in my choices.

It is imperative to think through any investment I am contemplating. A thorough study, which carefully considers the projected benefits and potential risks, will guide my decisions. This thoughtful approach will allow me to accurately evaluate the investment in question. Once I have thoroughly analyzed and understood the crucial aspects, I will be ready to make the investment without fear, backed by the preparation and knowledge I have gained, thus setting me on the road to success and achieving the wealth and happiness I crave.

DOCEAVA RULE

SE CAUTO

C aution is an art, do not be fooled by others, as most people try, by all means possible, to get the most out of you for their benefit.

When they praise your ear and your person. Be cautious.

Plan your work well, trace your definite route, do not leave anything to chance or to chance, on the contrary, whatever you undertake or do, do it well, do not do it half-heartedly or badly, because that will only bring you problems, while if you do everything well you will have wealth and happiness.

It supports the effort of the work, as if it were a game.

Remember that perseverance is stronger than intelligence, if you want to succeed in life or in the business you undertake. But this, plan it with caution, do not leave it to chance.

When people have achieved wealth and happiness, they show that they have always been cautious in undertaking a business or job.

Have faith in your work, be a believer in yourself, in what you do or develop, in what you sell or manufacture.

The secret to success is work, which must be done with love, selflessness, passion and joy.

Reflect on what you do or perform, make it worthy of you, so that others will thank you for it.

Remember your failures, so as not to incur them again, make the most of them, since these experiences will help you to turn them into triumphs and your time into wealth and happiness.

Study your path and your desired end, and if necessary, retrace it again and again until you perfect it, including the caution to achieve the desired success.

Always keep in mind that the unsuccessful ones have never been cautious in developing their work.

They are people who don't care what others think of them, don't be like that.

"I want to succeed and for my work to be recognized by others, for my name to be proclaimed everywhere as an achiever, not as a failure."

"I want my family, wife and children, if I have them or will have them, to be proud of me, and I will only achieve this with my work and my time."

"I want to be worthy of my family and
those around me."

"I must have faith that my triumphs are
coming, but, for this, it is necessary to
redouble my work effort, with the
corresponding caution"

Believe in yourself and nothing will be impossible, no matter how many obstacles you find to reach the desired goal, which is success, wealth and happiness, always think carefully to do your work, do it well, do it with the greatest possible perfection, so, you will obtain the desired triumphs and you will reach wealth and happiness.

You have the right to it, the only one who takes away that right is you, and no one else but you.

In such a virtue, it is necessary that you make a resolution to be a winner and not a loser.

Be cautious in what you undertake so that you do not suffer defeat.

Analyze, as many times as necessary, each of these simple Rules to be rich and happy.

Do not keep them in the drawer of oblivion, they are necessary every day, so that you can be rich and happy.

I hope they will serve you in your life's journey and that you will be another winner in this world.

www.ingramcontent.com/pod-product-compliance
Lightning Source LLC
Chambersburg PA
CBHW062302290526
45794CB00006B/2658